TODAY'S SPORTS STARS
Lamar Jackson
Football Star

by Derek Moon

FOCUS READERS®
BEACON

www.focusreaders.com

Copyright © 2026 by Focus Readers®, Mendota Heights, MN 55120. All rights reserved. No part of this book may be reproduced or utilized in any form or by any means without written permission from the publisher.

Focus Readers is distributed by North Star Editions:
sales@northstareditions.com | 888-417-0195

Produced for Focus Readers by Red Line Editorial.

Photographs ©: Terrance Williams/AP Images, cover, 1; Joe Robbins/AP Images, 4, 29; Rob Carr/Getty Images Sport/Getty Images, 7, 17, 20; Shutterstock Images, 8; Michael Hickey/Getty Images Sport/Getty Images, 11; Grant Halverson/Getty Images Sport/Getty Images, 13; Joe Robbins/Getty Images Sport/Getty Images, 14; Will Newton/Getty Images Sport/Getty Images, 18; Patrick Smith/Getty Images Sport/Getty Images, 23; Greg Fiume/Getty Images Sport/Getty Images, 25; Red Line Editorial, 27

Library of Congress Cataloging-in-Publication Data
Names: Moon, Derek author
Title: Lamar Jackson: football star / by Derek Moon.
Description: Mendota Heights, MN: Focus Readers, 2026. | Series: Today's sports stars | Includes index. | Audience: Grades 2-3
Identifiers: LCCN 2025009912 (print) | LCCN 2025009913 (ebook) | ISBN 9798889985938 hardcover | ISBN 9798889986195 paperback | ISBN 9798889986102 pdf | ISBN 9798889986027 ebook
Subjects: LCSH: Jackson, Lamar, 1997---Juvenile literature | Quarterbacks (Football)--United States--Biography--Juvenile literature | LCGFT: Biographies
Classification: LCC GV939.J29 M66 2026 (print) | LCC GV939.J29 (ebook) | DDC 796.332092--dc23/eng/20250407
LC record available at https://lccn.loc.gov/2025009912
LC ebook record available at https://lccn.loc.gov/2025009913

Printed in the United States of America
Mankato, MN
082025

About the Author

Derek Moon is an author and avid Stratego player who lives in Watertown, Massachusetts, with his wife and daughter.

Table of Contents

CHAPTER 1

Doing It All 5

CHAPTER 2

Taking Flight 9

CHAPTER 3

Ready to Go 15

CHAPTER 4

Dual-Threat Superstar 21

At-a-Glance Map • 26

Focus Questions • 28

Glossary • 30

To Learn More • 31

Index • 32

CHAPTER 1

Doing It All

Lamar Jackson took the **snap** and scanned the field. His Baltimore Ravens faced second-and-five. The quarterback quickly spotted an open receiver. But his pass never got there.

Lamar Jackson looks for a receiver during a January 2024 playoff game.

A Kansas City Chiefs defender tipped the ball. It floated into the air. A Chiefs safety tried to grab it. But he was too late. Jackson had read the play perfectly. He raced ahead to catch his own pass. Then he bolted 13 yards for a first down. The heads-up play kept the Ravens' drive alive.

> **Did You Know?**
> The ESPY Awards named Jackson's catch the best play of the year.

Jackson catches his own pass in a playoff game against the Kansas City Chiefs.

Baltimore ended up losing the January 2024 **playoff** game. But Jackson's skills were clear. He finished the season with his second Most Valuable Player (MVP) Award.

CHAPTER 2

Taking Flight

Lamar Jackson was born on January 7, 1997. He grew up in Pompano Beach, Florida. The city is just north of Miami. Lamar began playing football around age seven.

Pompano Beach, Florida, lies along the Atlantic Ocean.

Soon after, Lamar's dad died. It was a very difficult time. But his mom made sure he stayed strong.

From the start, Lamar's football skills were obvious. He could both run and pass the football. He was also a perfectionist. He practiced until he got things just right. As a kid, Lamar often scored six touchdowns in a game.

Many colleges wanted Lamar to play for them. However, most wanted him to try other positions.

Lamar Jackson scores during the first game of the 2016 season.

Lamar was **determined** to play quarterback. The University of Louisville gave him that chance.

Jackson showed promise early. But few people knew about him going into his sophomore season.

That changed quickly. In the 2016 opener, Jackson tossed six touchdown passes. He ran for two more scores.

Jackson ended the season with 51 total touchdowns. He also racked up 5,114 total yards. It was one of the best **dual-threat** seasons

Did You Know?
Jackson became the youngest player ever to win the Heisman Trophy. He was just 19 years, 337 days old.

 In a 2017 game, Jackson recorded three passing touchdowns and three rushing touchdowns.

ever. Jackson won the Heisman Trophy. That award is given to the best player in college football.

Jackson piled up even more yards in 2017. After that, his next step was clear. He headed to the National Football League (NFL).

CHAPTER 3
Ready to Go

Lamar Jackson had shown he had a strong arm. However, some NFL teams focused more on his athleticism. He could burst past defenders. Many teams pictured him doing that as a receiver.

Lamar Jackson showed off his passing skills before the 2018 NFL Draft.

Jackson never considered it. He knew he could succeed as a quarterback. The Baltimore Ravens agreed. They took him in the first round of the 2018 NFL **Draft**.

Baltimore already had a good quarterback. Joe Flacco had led the Ravens to a Super Bowl title a few years earlier. However, Flacco injured his hip during the 2018 season. Jackson stepped in. He was a natural. He led the Ravens to six wins in seven games.

Jackson's first NFL start came on November 18, 2018, against the Cincinnati Bengals.

After that, the team went all in on Jackson. He had passed well as a **rookie**. But he was a game changer when he ran. The Ravens updated their playbook.

 In Week 6 of the 2019 season, Jackson rushed for a career-high 152 yards.

They built everything around Jackson's strengths.

The result was a breakout 2019 season. Jackson threw an 83-yard touchdown in the opener. It was one of 36 touchdown passes that season. No quarterback had more. Jackson also ran for 1,206 yards. That set a record for quarterbacks. Meanwhile, Baltimore won a team-record 14 games. Afterward, all 50 voters picked Jackson as the league's MVP.

Did You Know?

Jackson made *Madden NFL* history in 2019. The video game rated his speed as 96 of 100. It was the highest rating ever for a quarterback.

CHAPTER 4

Dual-Threat Superstar

The 2019 season had shown Lamar Jackson's ability. And he remained an **elite** quarterback. Jackson had a solid 2020 season. However, injuries shortened his 2021 and 2022 seasons.

Lamar Jackson flips into the end zone during a 2021 game against the Chiefs.

The Ravens still believed in Jackson, though. They made him the highest-paid player in the NFL. And in 2023, Jackson stepped up with his best passing season yet. He also ran for 821 yards.

Baltimore had some skilled receivers and running backs. But

Did You Know?

Jackson started a group in 2018. It focuses on helping people learn about the importance of **mental health**.

Jackson had four total touchdowns in a January 2024 playoff win against the Houston Texans.

none of them were game changers. That meant the Ravens relied on Jackson to power the offense. Baltimore won a league-best 13 games. Jackson also won his second MVP Award.

Jackson was private off the field. But with his team, he was known as a great leader. Teammates and coaches trusted him. In turn, the Ravens kept giving him more freedom. Jackson responded in 2024 with the best dual-threat season of all time. He had always thrived on the run. Now he was a historically good passer, too.

The Ravens won 12 games. Then Jackson led them to a playoff win. However, they lost in the next

In 2024, Jackson became the first NFL quarterback to top 4,000 passing yards and 800 rushing yards in a season.

round. It was a disappointing finish to a great season. There was no doubting his talent, though. Ravens fans believed he could soon take the team to the next level.

AT-A-GLANCE MAP

Lamar Jackson

- Height: 6 feet, 2 inches (188 cm)
- Weight: 205 pounds (93 kg)
- Birth date: January 7, 1997
- Birthplace: Pompano Beach, Florida
- High schools: Santaluces Community High School (Lantana, Florida); Boynton Beach Community High School (Boynton Beach, Florida)
- College: University of Louisville (Louisville, Kentucky) (2015–17)
- NFL team: Baltimore Ravens (2018–)
- Major awards: Heisman Trophy (2016); Pro Bowl (2019, 2021, 2023, 2024); NFL MVP (2019, 2023)

Focus Questions

Write your answers on a separate piece of paper.

1. Write a few sentences explaining the main ideas of Chapter 2.
2. Why do you think Lamar Jackson was determined to keep playing quarterback instead of becoming a receiver?
3. How old was Jackson when he won the Heisman Trophy?
    - A. 18 years old
    - B. 19 years old
    - C. 20 years old
4. Why did the Ravens give Jackson more and more freedom on the field?
    - A. The coaches were unsure of his strengths and weaknesses.
    - B. He never followed the playbook anyway.
    - C. They trusted he would make good decisions.

5. What does **scanned** mean in this book?

*Lamar Jackson took the snap and **scanned** the field. His Baltimore Ravens faced second-and-five. The quarterback quickly spotted an open receiver.*

- **A.** made a recording
- **B.** ran quickly
- **C.** looked around

6. What does **perfectionist** mean in this book?

*He was also a **perfectionist**. He practiced until he got things just right.*

- **A.** someone who works hard to do everything well
- **B.** someone who can only perform when conditions are right
- **C.** someone who struggles to do a good job

Answer key on page 32.

Glossary

determined
Not wanting to let anyone stop you from doing something.

draft
A system that allows teams to acquire new players coming into a league.

dual-threat
Able to both run and pass the ball well.

elite
The best of the best.

mental health
How well or unwell someone's mind is, including their emotions and thinking.

playoff
Having to do with a series of games played after the regular season to decide which team will be the champion.

rookie
A professional athlete in his or her first year.

snap
The start of each play when the center passes the ball back to the quarterback.

To Learn More

BOOKS

Adamson, Thomas K. *Baltimore Ravens*. Bellwether Media, 2024.

Graves, Will. *Baltimore Ravens*. Apex Editions, 2025.

Leed, Percy. *Meet Lamar Jackson: Baltimore Ravens Superstar*. Lerner Publications, 2025.

NOTE TO EDUCATORS

Visit **www.focusreaders.com** to find lesson plans, activities, links, and other resources related to this title.

Index

B
Baltimore Ravens, 5–7, 16–19, 22–25

D
draft, 16

E
ESPY Awards, 6

F
Flacco, Joe, 16

H
Heisman Trophy, 12–13

K
Kansas City Chiefs, 6

L
Louisville, University of, 11

M
Madden NFL, 19
mental health, 22
Most Valuable Player (MVP) Award, 7, 19, 23

N
National Football League (NFL), 13, 15, 22

P
playoffs, 7, 24
Pompano Beach, Florida, 9

S
Super Bowl, 16